CHORDS

COUNTRY SHEET MUSIC HITS

MW01011772

Product Line Manager: Carol Cuellar
Project Manager: Zobeida Pérez
Cover Design: Joe Klucar

© 2003 WARNER BROS. PUBLICATIONS
All Rights Reserved

CONTENTS

I HOPE YOU DANCE

Words and Music by
MARK D. SANDERS and
TIA SILLERS

Moderately slow ♩ = 80

hope you nev-er lose____ your sense of won - der.____ You get your fill____

2. *See additional lyrics*

I Hope You Dance - 5 - 1

4

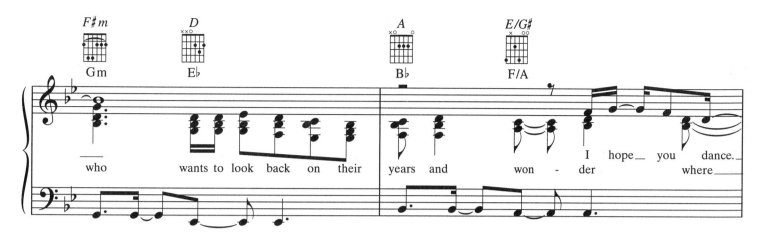

Repeat ad lib. and fade

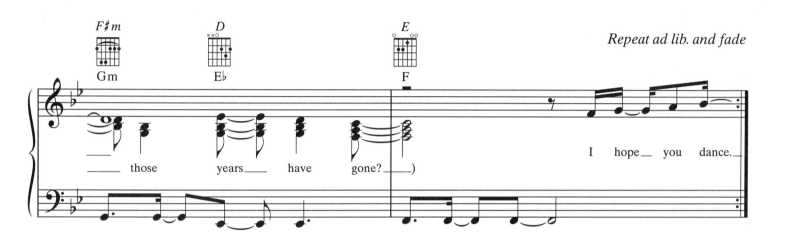

Verse 2:
I hope you never fear those mountains in the distance,
Never settle for the path of least resistance.
Livin' might mean takin' chances but they're worth takin'.
Lovin' might be a mistake but it's worth makin'.

Chorus 2:
Don't let some hell-bent heart leave you bitter.
When you come close to sellin' out, reconsider.
Give the heavens above more than just a passing glance.
And when you get the choice to sit it out or dance,...
(To Chorus 3:)

AMAZED

Words and Music by
MARV GREEN, AIMEE MAYO
and CHRIS LINDSEY

Verse 2:
The smell of your skin,
The taste of your kiss,
The way you whisper in the dark.
Your hair all around me,
Baby, you surround me;
You touch every place in my heart.
Oh, it feels like the first time every time.
I wanna spend the whole night in your eyes.
(To Chorus:)

BECAUSE YOU LOVE ME

Words and Music by
KOSTAS and JOHN SCOTT SHERRILL

Because You Love Me - 3 - 1

Verse 3:
Instrumental solo ad lib.
(To Bridge:)

Verse 4:
I believe in things unseen;
I believe in the message of a dream.
And I believe in what you are
Because you love me.

Verse 5:
With all my heart
And all my soul,
I'm loving you and I never will let go.
And every day I let it show
Because you love me.
(To Coda)

BREATHE

Words and Music by
STEPHANIE BENTLEY
and HOLLY LAMAR

Slowly ♩ = 60

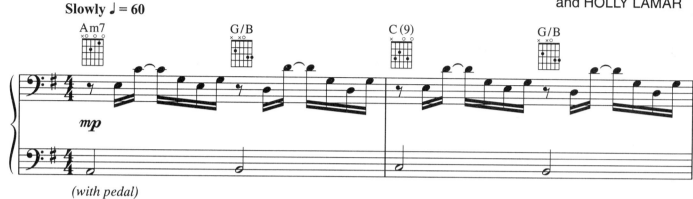

(with pedal)

Verse 1:

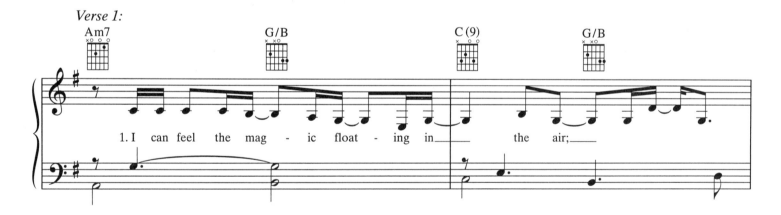

1. I can feel the mag - ic float - ing in ___ the air; ___

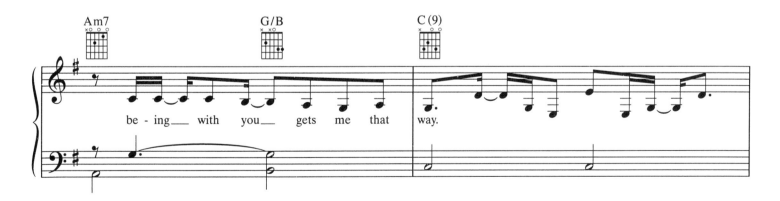

be - ing ___ with you ___ gets me that way.

Breathe - 5 - 1

16

Chorus:

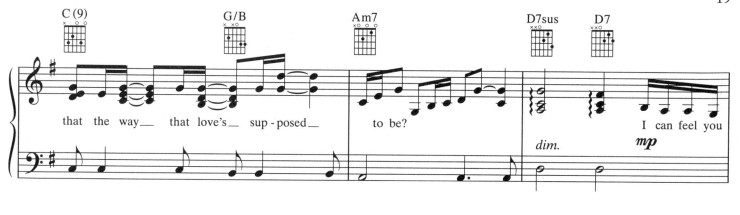

that the way___ that love's___ sup-posed___ to be?

dim.   *mp*

I can feel you

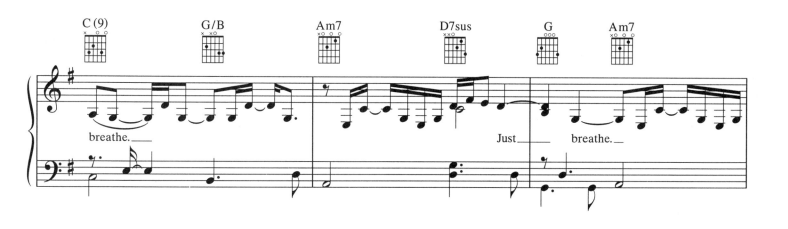

breathe.___   Just___ breathe.___

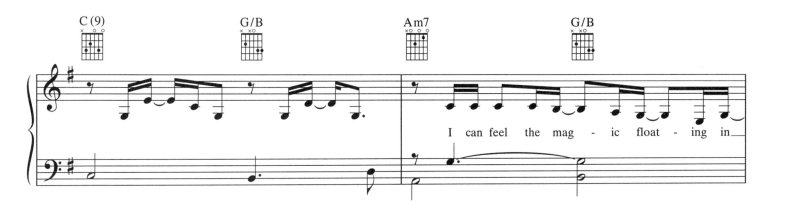

I can feel the mag - ic float - ing in

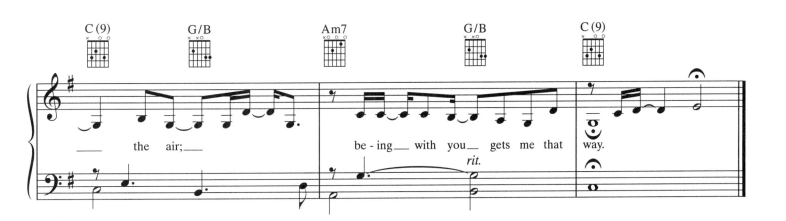

___ the air;___   be - ing___ with you___ gets me that way.

rit.

CONCRETE ANGEL

Words and Music by
STEPHANIE BENTLEY and
ROB CROSBY

1. She walks to school with the
2.3.4. *See additional lyrics*

lunch she packed._____ No - bod - y knows what she's_____ hold - in' back._____

Verse 2:
The teacher wonders but she doesn't ask.
It's hard to see the pain behind the mask.
Bearing the burden of a secret storm,
Sometimes she wishes she was never born.
(To Chorus:)

Verse 3:
Somebody cries in the middle of the night.
The neighbors hear, but they turn out the light.
A fragile soul caught in the hands of fate,
When morning comes, it'll be too late.
(To Chorus:)

Verse 4:
A statue stands in a shaded place,
An angel girl with an upturned face.
A name is written on a polished rock
A broken heart that the world forgot.
(To Chorus:)

THE DANCE

Words and Music by
TONY ARATA

The Dance - 3 - 1

THE DEVIL WENT DOWN TO GEORGIA

Words and Music by
CHARLIE DANIELS, JOHN THOMAS CRAIN, JR.,
WILLIAM JOEL DiGREGORIO, FRED LAROY EDWARDS,
CHARLES FRED HAYWARD and JAMES WAINWRIGHT MARSHALL

The Devil Went Down to Georgia - 13 - 1

28

hell's broke loose in Geor - gia and___ the dev - il deals the cards. And

if you win, you get this shin - y fid - dle made of gold. But

if you lose, the dev - il gets your soul._____

73 *Solo:*

(Violin)

32

81 Verse 4:

dev-il o-pened up his case and he said, "I'll start this show." and fire___

___ flew from his fin-ger-tips as he ros-ined up his bow.___ And he

pulled the bow a-cross the strings and it made an e-vil hiss. Then a

34

Bridge:

Fire on the moun-tain; run,___ boys, run. *(Violin)* The

dev-il's in the House of the Ris-ing Sun. *(Violin)*

Chick-en in the bread-pan, pick-in' out dough. *(Violin)*

Gran-ny, does your dog bite? No, child, no. *(Violin)*

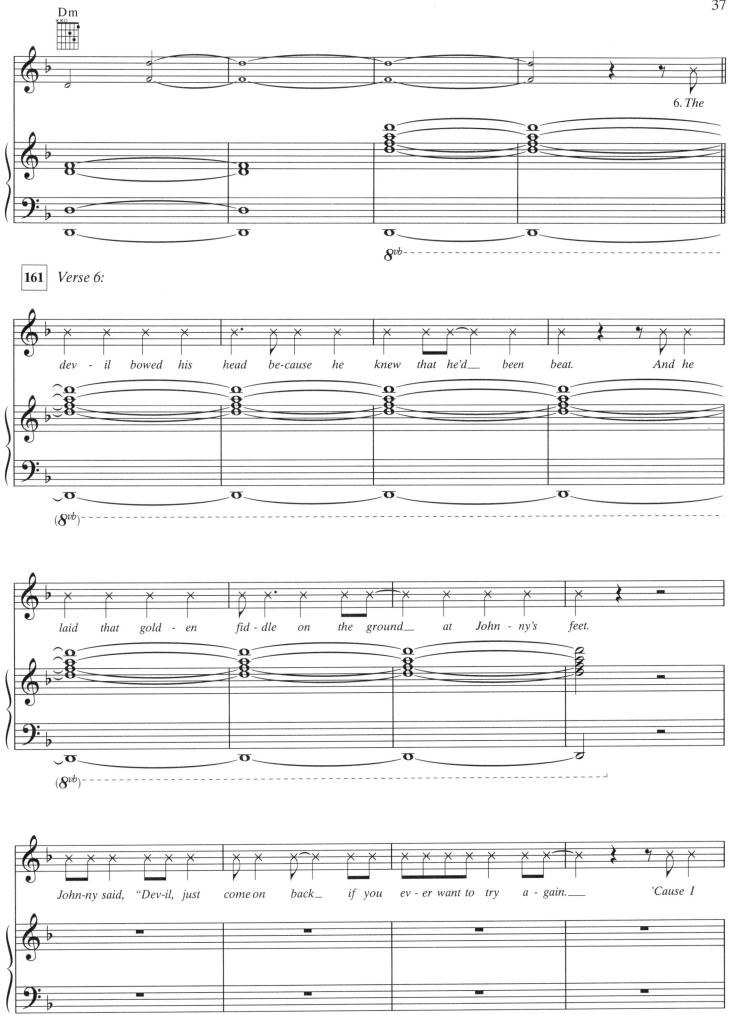

6. The

161 *Verse 6:*

dev - il bowed his head be-cause he knew that he'd___ been beat. And he

laid that gold - en fid - dle on the ground___ at John - ny's feet.

John-ny said, "Dev-il, just come on back___ if you ev - er want to try a - gain.___ 'Cause I

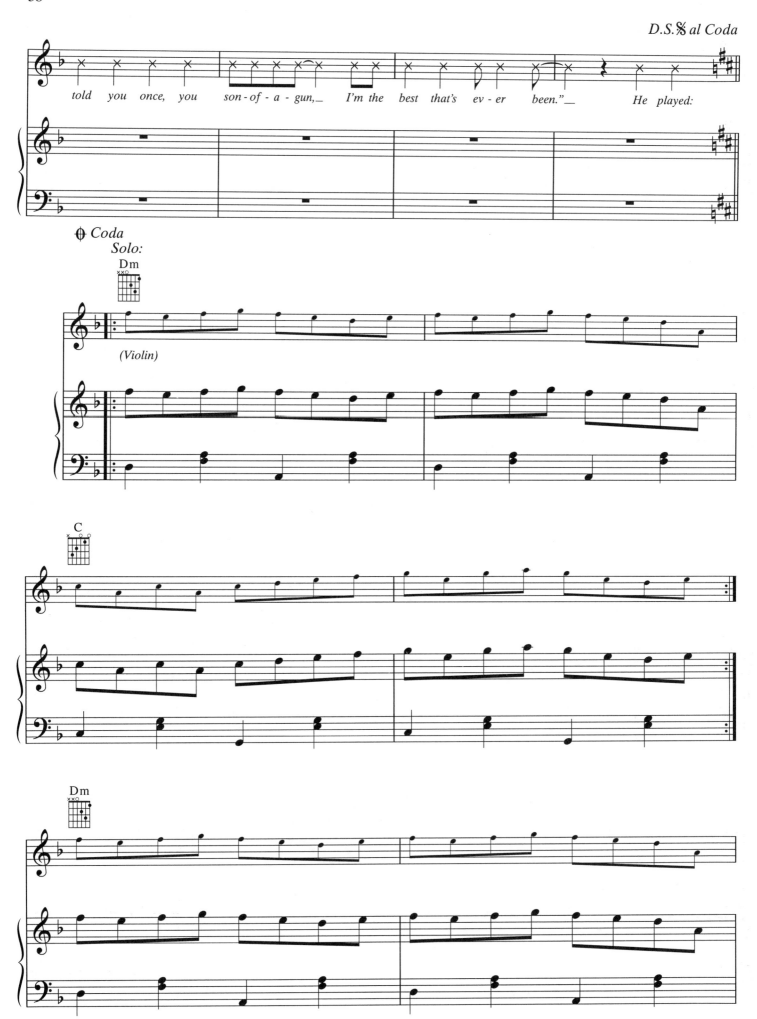

FROM THIS MOMENT ON

Words and Music by
SHANIA TWAIN and R.J. LANGE

From This Moment On - 7 - 1

42

46

From This Moment On - 7 - 7

GO REST HIGH ON THAT MOUNTAIN

Words and Music by
VINCE GILL

Slowly, in Gospel style

Go Rest High on That Mountain - 3 - 1

48

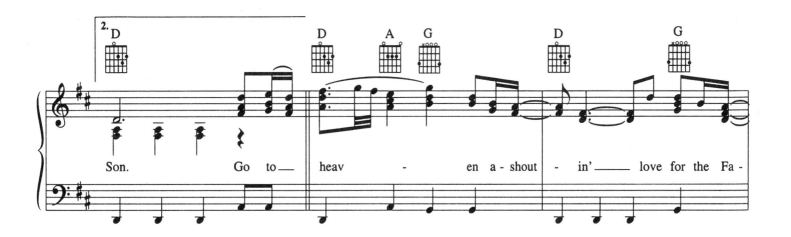

Son. Go to heav- en a-shout- in' love for the Fa-

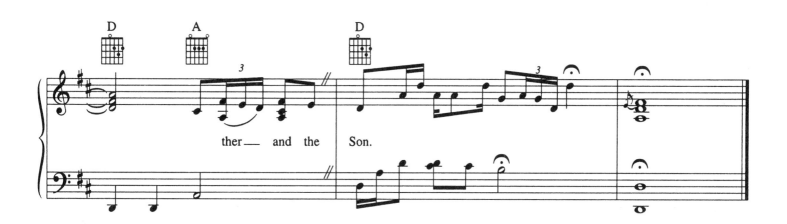

ther and the Son.

Additional lyrics

2. Oh, how we cried the day you left us,
   We gathered 'round your grave to grieve.
   I wish I could see the angels' faces
   When they hear your sweet voice sing.
   (To Chorus)

HOLES IN THE FLOOR OF HEAVEN

Words and Music by
STEVE WARINER and BILLY KIRSCH

52

Verse 2:
Seasons come and seasons go,
Nothing stays the same.
I grew up, fell in love,
Met a girl who took my name.
Year by year we made a life
In this sleepy, little town.
I thought we'd grow old together.
Lord, I sure do miss her now.
(To Chorus:)

Verse 3:
Well, my little girl is twenty-three,
I walk her down the aisle.
It's a shame her mom can't be here now
To see her lovely smile.
They throw the rice, I catch her eye
As the rain starts coming down.
She takes my hand, says, "Daddy, don't be sad,
'Cause I know Mama's watching now."
(To Chorus:)

From the Touchstone Motion Picture "CON AIR"

HOW DO I LIVE

Words and Music by
DIANE WARREN

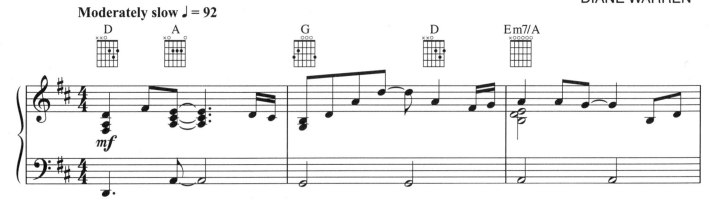

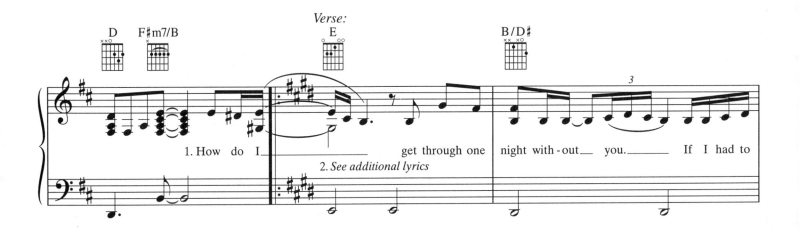

1. How do I _____ get through one night with-out_ you._____ If I had to

2. *See additional lyrics*

live with-out_ you,_ what kind of life would that be?_ Oh,_ I,_____ I need you in my

arms, need you_ to hold._ You're my world, my heart,_ my soul._ If you ev - er leave,

How Do I Live - 4 - 1

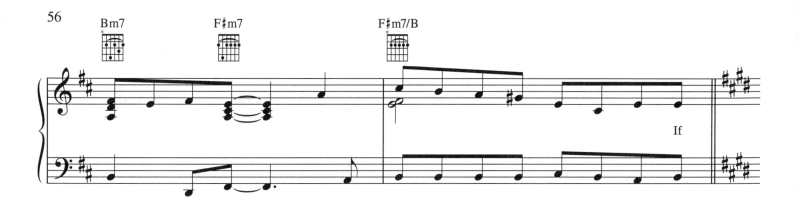

If

you ev - er leave,_____ ba - by, you would take a - way___ ev - 'ry - thing.___

Need you with me._____ Ba - by, 'coz you know that you're ev - 'ry - thing___

D.S. % al Coda

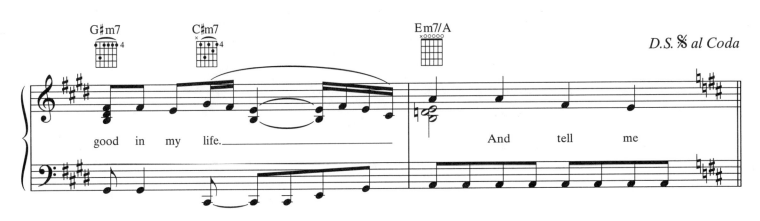

good in my life._____ And tell me

⊕ *Coda*

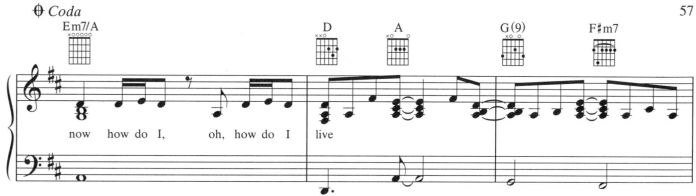

now how do I, oh, how do I live

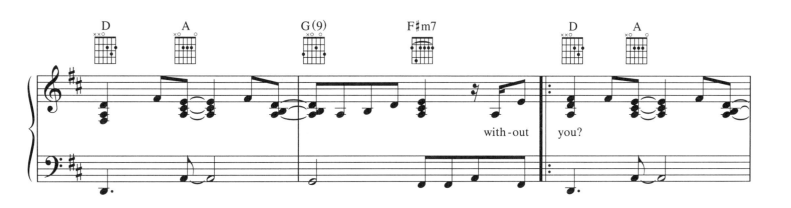

with-out you?

Repeat ad lib. and fade
(vocal 1st time only)

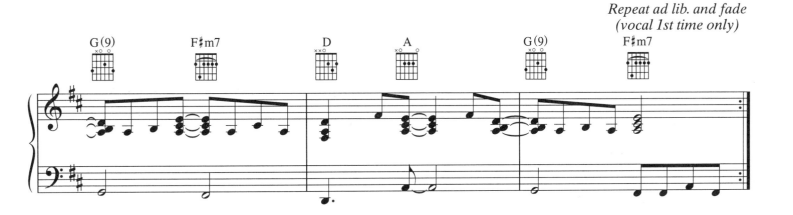

Verse 2:
Without you, there'd be no sun in my sky,
There would be no love in my life,
There'd be no world left for me.
And I, baby, I don't know what I would do,
I'd be lost if I lost you.
If you ever leave,
Baby, you would take away everything real in my life.
And tell me now…
(To Chorus:)

I COULD NOT ASK FOR MORE

Words and Music by
DIANE WARREN

I CROSS MY HEART

Words and Music by
STEVE DORFF and ERIC KAZ

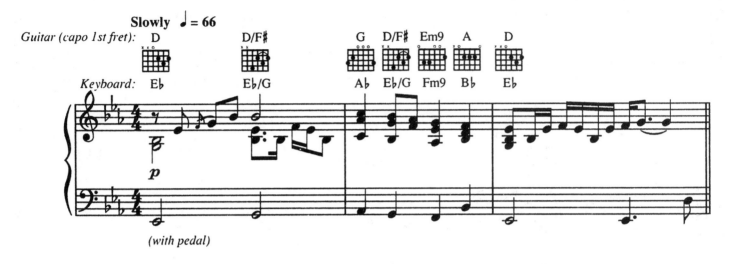

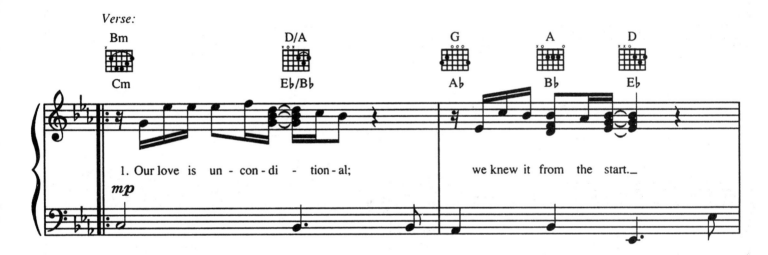

1. Our love is un-con-di-tion-al; we knew it from the start.

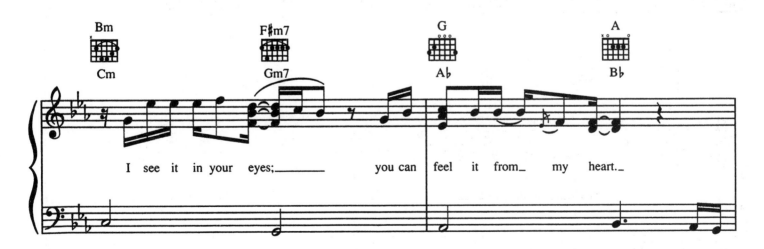

I see it in your eyes; you can feel it from my heart.

I Cross My Heart - 4 - 1

64

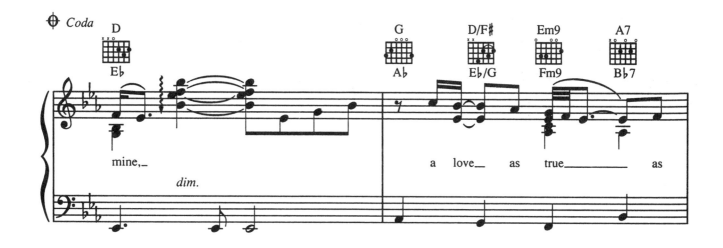

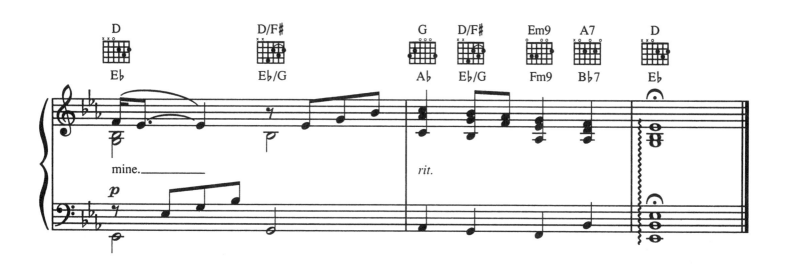

Verse 2:
You will always be the miracle
That makes my life complete;
And as long as there's a breath in me,
I'll make yours just as sweet.
As we look into the future,
It's as far as we can see,
So let's make each tomorrow
Be the best that it can be.
(To Chorus:)

THIS KISS

Words and Music by
ROBIN LERNER, ANNIE ROBOFF
and BETH NIELSEN CHAPMAN

Moderately, with double-time feel ♩ = 64

Verse:

1. I don't want an-oth-er heart-break. I don't need an-oth-er turn to cry,_____ no.
2. Cin-der-el-la said to Snow White, "How does love get so off course?"_____ Oh.

I don't want to learn the hard way. Ba-by,
All I want-ed was a white knight with a

hel - lo, oh no, good - bye.
good heart, soft touch, fast horse.

This Kiss - 4 - 1

68

I SWEAR

Words and Music by
GARY BAKER and FRANK MYERS

72

Additional lyrics

2. I'll give you everything I can,
    I'll build your dreams with these two hands,
    And we'll hang some memories on the wall.
    And when there's silver in your hair,
    You won't have to ask if I still care,
    'Cause as time turns the page my love won't age at all.
    (To Chorus)

I'LL BE

Words and Music by
DIANE WARREN

76

Verse 2:
And when you're there with no one there to hold,
I'll be the arms that reach for you.
And when you feel your faith is running low,
I'll be there to believe in you.
When all you find are lies,
I'll be the truth you need.
When you need someone to run to,
You can run to me.
(To Chorus:)

I'M ALREADY THERE

Words and Music by
GARY BAKER, FRANK J. MYERS
and RICHIE McDONALD

I'm Already There - 5 - 1

I'M MOVIN' ON

Words and Music by
D. VINCENT WILLIAMS
and PHILLIP WHITE

I'm Movin' On - 6 - 1

THE KEEPER OF THE STARS

Words and Music by
KAREN STALEY, DANNY MAYO and DICKIE LEE

Slowly ♩ = 76

(with pedal)

Verse:

1. It was no ac - ci - dent,_ me find - ing
2. Soft moon-light on your face,_ oh how_ you

you. Some-one had a hand_ in it_
shine! It takes my_ breath_ a - way_

long be - fore_ we ev - er_ knew.
just to look_ in - to your_ eyes.

The Keeper of the Stars - 4 - 1

ON THE SIDE OF ANGELS

Words and Music by
GERRY HOUSE and GARY BURR

SOMETHING THAT WE DO

Guitar originally recorded
in alternate tuning (open D)
w/capo at 5th fret:

⑥ = D ③ = F#
⑤ = A ② = A
④ = D ① = D

Words and Music by
CLINT BLACK and SKIP EWING

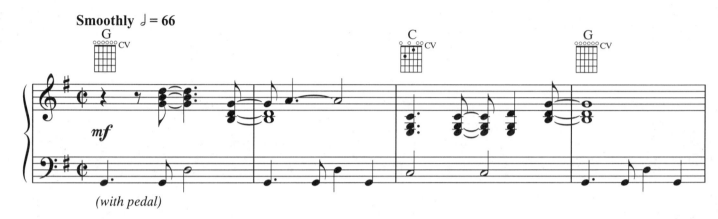

(with pedal)

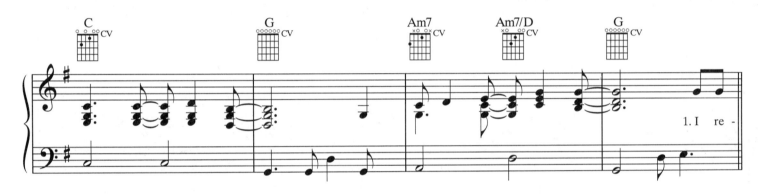

1. I re-

Verses 1 & 2:

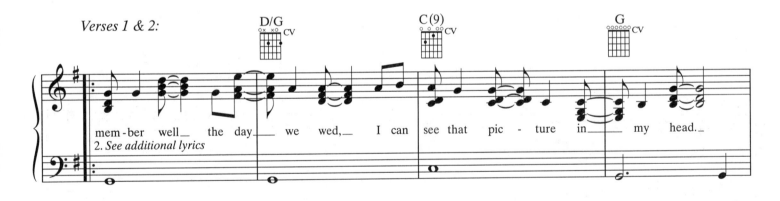

mem-ber well the day we wed, I can see that pic-ture in my head.
2. See additional lyrics

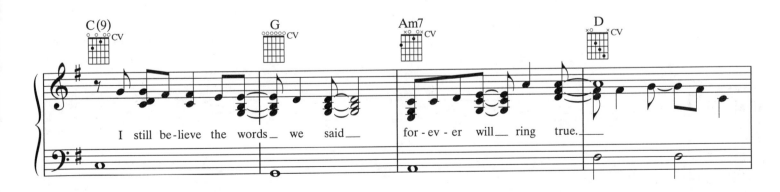

I still be-lieve the words we said for-ev-er will ring true.

Something That We Do - 5 - 1

98

Something That We Do - 5 - 3

Verse 2:
It's holding tight, lettin' go,
It's flyin' high and layin' low.
Let your strongest feelings show
And your weakness, too.
It's a little and a lot to ask,
An endless and a welcome task.
Love isn't something that we have,
It's something that we do.
(To Bridge:)

WHEN YOU SAY NOTHING AT ALL

Words and Music by
PAUL OVERSTREET and DON SCHLITZ

When You Say Nothing at All - 3 - 1

THERE YOU ARE

Words and Music by
MARK D. SANDERS, BOB DiPIERO
and ED HILL

There You Are - 4 - 1

Verse 2:
There you are standing in a crowded room.
There you are, the earth and I'm the moon.
My desire is to stand by the fire
That burns inside of you.
(To Chorus:)

COME ON OVER

Words and Music by
SHANIA TWAIN and R.J. LANGE

Moderate calypso rock ♩ = 76

1. Get a life,

Come On Over - 6 - 1

YOU'RE STILL THE ONE

Words and Music by
SHANIA TWAIN and R.J. LANGE

Verse 2:
Ain't nothin' better,
We beat the odds together.
I'm glad we didn't listen.
Look at what we would be missin'.
(To Bridge:)